The Journey

Taking your next steps

Copyright © 2021 Mark Greenwood

First published in 2005. Revised and reprinted in 2011. This revised edition first published in 2021.

revmarkgreenwood.com

Published for Mark Greenwood
by Verité CM Ltd
Worthing, BN12 4BG, UK
veritecm.com

The right of Mark Greenwood to be identified as the author of this work has been asserted by him in accordance with the Copyright, Designs and Patents Act 1988.

ISBN: 978-1-914388-22-4

All rights reserved. No part of this publication may be reproduced or transmitted in any form or by any means, electronic or mechanical, including photocopy, recording or any information storage and retrieval system, without permission in writing from the author.

.

British Library Cataloguing Data

A catalogue record of this book is available from The British Library.

Scripture quotations are taken from The Holy Bible, New International Version (Anglicised edition), copyright © 1979, 1984, 2011 by Biblica. Used by permission of Hodder & Stoughton Publishers, an Hachette UK company.

All rights reserved.

Printed in England

Designed by Ashdown Creative

The Journey

Taking your next steps

MARK GREENWOOD

Acknowledgements

Special thanks to Ashdown Creative, Verité CM Ltd and Louise Stenhouse for all your work getting this published.

Thanks also to Brigitte, Chloé, Norman, Tim, Graham, Zoe, Phil and Nitasha for sharing your journey to help others on their journey.

Welcome to
The Journey

Let me introduce you to Big Yes, Little Yes, Healthy Maybe.

Big Yes

Many people have said a 'Big Yes' to God and decided to follow him and his ways. They have asked God to forgive them for leaving him out of their life and for doing their own thing. They have embraced Jesus' death on the cross and his coming back to life, receiving his forgiveness and new life and, in so doing, understand that God wants them to make a difference in the world as they connect with him.

Little Yes

Many people have made an intentional decision to find out more, to investigate whether Christianity is true. Sometimes it's because they are thinking about God and sometimes it's simply because they are thinking about life.

Healthy Maybe

Many people consider themselves open minded but don't always apply that stance to Christianity. A Healthy Maybe is someone who is willing to become open minded about Christianity, or if they are already open minded, they make a commitment to stay so and may be willing to chat about it openly.

This book is for those who have said a 'Big Yes' to God. It's to help you in the early stages of your new-found faith. If you are a 'Little Yes' or 'Healthy Maybe' it will still benefit you – in particular, the stories of those in each of the daily sections – but I would encourage you to speak to whoever gave you this book so they can help you on your journey. If you don't know the person then you can contact me via my website and I can help you. It's on the back cover.

To those who are 'Big Yes', you will have questions about the Christian faith now you've given your life over to God, and that's a good thing.

> C.S. Lewis said, 'One of the reasons it needs no special education to be a Christian is that Christianity is an education itself.'

The Christian life is a journey and, as with any journey, there are decisions, obstacles and uncertainties along the way. That's why it's good to ask questions so you keep making the right decisions and taking the right turnings.

There will never be a time on earth when you'll be perfect; that has to wait until you get to heaven. There will never be a time in your new Christian life that you will have learned everything – there is always something new to discover. What's important is that you keep going even when you feel discouraged and find it hard. That is also part of the learning and what develops the strength of your walk with God.

In each daily section of this guide you will read some words from me as well reading about different people's journeys. There are some words from the Bible and some prayers you can use until you feel confident with praying to God, as well as a space for you to add 'Your Thoughts' in whatever way you like to do that. You will also find a QR code which you can use to discover more.

Happy reading,

Mark

Mark Greenwood

DAY 1

Was it real or was it just me?

If you haven't thought this already, then you probably will very soon. You've just said a 'Big Yes' to God and as with any big decision you make in life, you can have doubts about whether or not you have made the right decision.

Not only is this true in everyday life but it's true in the spiritual life too. There are spiritual forces that don't want you to be a Christian. They try to make you doubt your forgiveness from God and the promise of heaven when you die. Know this: **it was real and it wasn't just you.**

Brigitte's Journey

When I became a Christian, I was expecting something dramatic to happen, but for me everything just came in stages. I found myself not gossiping or drinking as much and, instead, I began to feel overwhelmed with compassion for people around me who didn't know Jesus. I didn't notice these changes until I reflected back later. The Lord answered my prayers, giving me what I needed rather than what I wanted. He knew my heart; he knew I needed a relationship with him and worked in me through his Holy Spirit before I even recognised it!

Words from the Bible

> 'And this is the testimony: God has given us eternal life, and this life is in his Son. Whoever has the Son has life; whoever does not have the Son of God does not have life.'
>
> 1 John 5:11-12

We can know for sure that the journey we are on is real. If you have said yes to God and meant it, you are a Christian now, which means you have the Son and so you really do have new life with a real God. It's fantastic.

You will learn more about this the longer you are on the journey, so keep going.

Words to Pray

Thank you, God, that, because I have turned away from a life without you and chosen to follow you, I am now in you. Thank you that this means I have life. Help me to realise I have made a real decision to follow a real God. Amen.

10 The Journey

Your Thoughts

Scan on your smartphone or tablet to help you discover more.

DAY 2

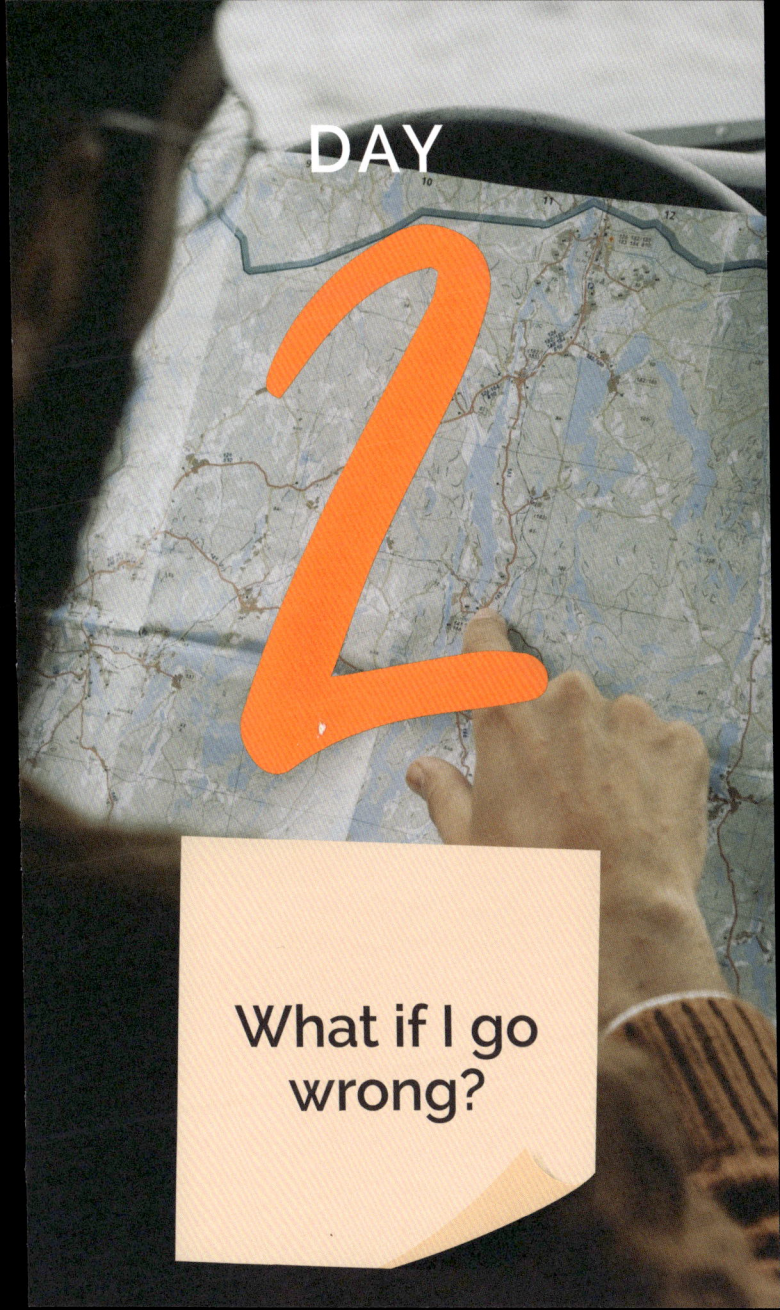

What if I go wrong?

You will!

Now I know that seems a bit harsh, but that's the reality. It is quite difficult being a Christian, but remember God wants to help you. The great thing is that Jesus died to forgive you when you didn't want to please God. Now that you do want to please God, if you trip up – and you will – God will forgive you. Ask God to help you turn away from what is wrong and embrace what is right.

Chloé's Journey

I've been a Christian for almost eight years and in that time I've learnt that 'going wrong' is inevitable. I've made so many mistakes along the way, but one thing I know is that the mistake shouldn't be the focus but how you deal with the mistake. God has been so gracious towards me, and forgives me even when I struggle to forgive myself. With each time I've gone wrong God has always taught me something new; he's always allowed me to grow as a follower of Jesus and he's helped me to hear his voice more clearly. Ultimately, we will 'go wrong' but with God's help we can always get back on track if we trust him.

Words from the Bible

> 'If we confess our sins, he is faithful and just and will forgive us our sins and purify us from all unrighteousness.'
>
> **1 John 1:9**

The journey starts with forgiveness and continues with forgiveness. God will always forgive us. It is important that we don't use this as an excuse and that we should do everything we can not to put ourselves in a place where we are tempted to do wrong. It's not always easy being a Christian but it's worth it.

You will learn more about this the longer you are on the journey, so keep going.

Words to Pray

God, I know I will go wrong, so please help me to know when I have gone wrong and to honestly confess my sin. Help me not to forget that you will always forgive me when I do. Please clean me up inside. Help me to live my life in a way that pleases you. Amen.

14 The Journey

Your Thoughts

Scan on your smartphone or tablet to help you discover more.

DAY 3

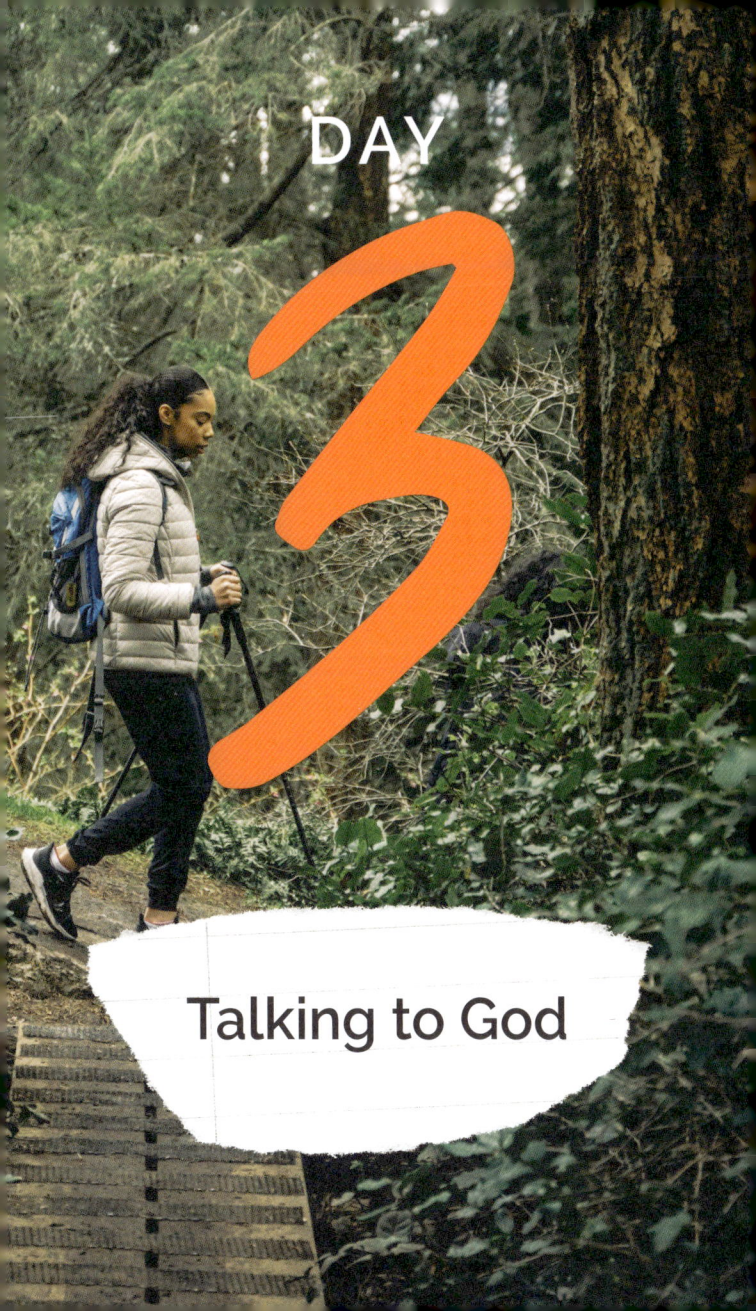

Talking to God

16 The Journey

Prayer is talking and listening to God. It may be a new thing to you but it's not something you should stress about. Start by thanking God for your new life. Thank him for forgiving you for leaving him out of your life and also that he has forgiven you for the wrong things you think, say and do. Thank Jesus for dying for you on the cross. Before long, prayer will become more natural to you. Talk to him about the challenges you are facing. Talk to him about where you feel you are in your life and faith.

Norman's Journey

I once went up a mountain summit of over 3,700 metres, part way by cable car but walking up to the peak. I found myself short of breath, having to keep stopping.

Why? Because at that height the air is thin and my body needs lots of air to function properly! In my Christian life, prayer is like the air my physical body needs. Without prayer I cannot function effectively as a Christian.

There is an old hymn which includes the line: 'Prayer is the Christian's vital breath, the Christian's native air.' I have found that to be true.

Words from the Bible

> 'Do not be anxious about anything, but in every situation, by prayer and petition, with thanksgiving, present your requests to God.'
>
> Philippians 4:6

God is always ready to listen. In fact, he is more willing to listen than we are to pray. Talk to God about everything on your journey, however insignificant or impossible you may feel it is.

You will learn more about this the longer you are on the journey, so keep going.

Words to Pray

Thank you, God, that I can talk to you and that you want to talk to me. Thank you that whether I am fluent in my words or I stumble over my words, you gladly listen to my prayer. Help me not to worry about anything, but instead to talk to you about everything. Amen.

18 The Journey

Your Thoughts

Scan on your smartphone or tablet to help you discover more.

DAY 4

Reading the manual

20 The Journey

God has given us the Bible as an instruction book – an owner's manual – which teaches us how to get the most out of life and our new-found faith. It teaches us how to live our lives in a way that pleases God. Doing what the Bible says not only pleases God but it brings fulfilment in our lives.

Because God made us, he alone knows how we work best and shows us this through the Bible. Whatever you face in your life, you can be sure that the Bible will have something to say that will help you deal with it.

Tim's Journey

I am notoriously useless at DIY. I'm one of those guys for whom putting up shelves is a serious challenge. On the rare occasion I purchase a new bit of flat-pack from IKEA... one thing I know for sure is this: I need the manual!

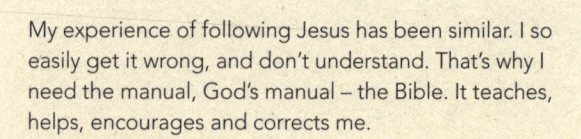

My experience of following Jesus has been similar. I so easily get it wrong, and don't understand. That's why I need the manual, God's manual – the Bible. It teaches, helps, encourages and corrects me.

These are God's precious words to me, and I can't build anything without them.

Words from the Bible

> 'Your word is a lamp for my feet, a light on my path.'
>
> Psalm 119:105

We don't have to stumble along like someone in the darkness looking for a light switch. God shows the way forward through his word, the Bible. It illuminates our journey often just a step at a time.

We can walk with confidence, putting one foot in front of the other knowing that we do so in a way that pleases God.

You will learn more about this the longer you are on the journey, so keep going.

Words to Pray

Thank you, God, for your word, the Bible. Thank you that it is your instruction book for life. Help me read it, understand it and allow it to guide me through my life as I now seek to follow you. Amen.

22 The Journey

Your Thoughts

Scan on your smartphone or tablet to help you discover more.

DAY 5

Journey with others

It's really important to worship God and to do it with other Christians. Now you're a Christian, it is essential to start going to church if you aren't already. Going to church is vital for your growth as a Christian and the benefit of meeting with other Christians is huge.

The community of believers is a place for you to find the answers to any questions you may have on your journey. It's a great place to be and you can come just as you are – you are accepted.

Graham's Journey

I was born into a Christian family and became a Christian when I was about eight years old. I spent my teenage years in the church but when we moved to the UK, although I very quickly got used to the English lifestyle I was far from God and other Christians. After my brother died in a car accident we started attending church regularly. I rededicated my life to God, realising what I had missed from my childhood. Everyone was friendly and made me very welcome – I couldn't wait for church on Sundays. I got involved in the church, helping wherever I could. I am now very honoured to be able to serve as an elder at church.

Journey with others 25

Words from the Bible

> 'And let us consider how we may spur one another on towards love and good deeds, not giving up meeting together, as some are in the habit of doing, but encouraging one another – and all the more as you see the Day approaching.'
>
> Hebrews 10:24-25

I feel at my best as a human when I am with those who are pulling in the same direction, cheering me on as we journey together. Don't travel alone; do it with like-minded Christians on the same journey, trying to live life God's way.

You will learn more about this the longer you are on the journey, so keep going.

Words to Pray

God, help me to meet together with other believers to worship you.

May I be encouraged by them and, in turn, let me encourage them. Help me get to know my new family. Amen.

Your Thoughts

Scan on your smartphone or tablet to help you discover more.

DAY 6

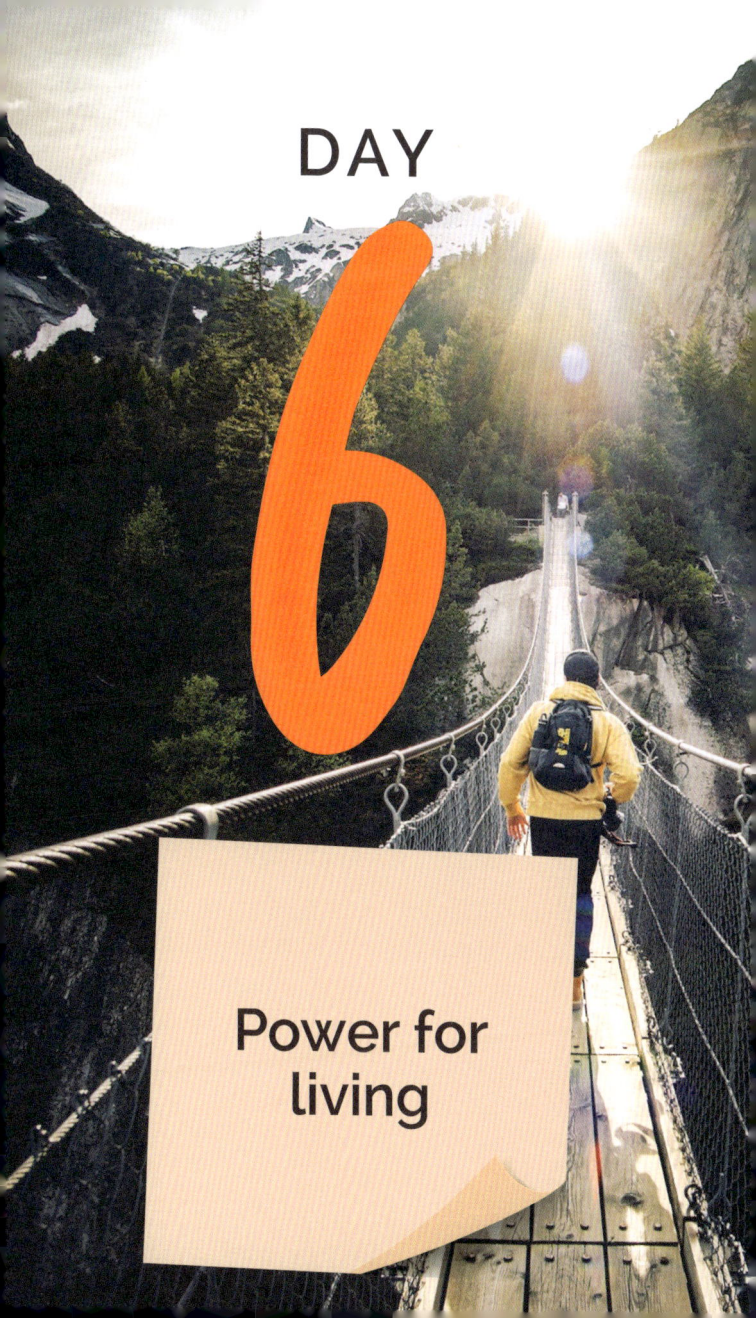

Power for living

When you become a Jesus follower God comes to live in you through the Holy Spirit, showing you how to live as well as empowering you to live as a Christian. It can be quite difficult getting your head around this at times but that's okay – God is sometimes a mystery.

There are times when you feel God and there are times when you don't, but what you can know is that he is living in you by the Holy Spirit. Ask other Christians to explain more about him to you as well as praying for you to experience him.

Zoe's Journey

I was born in a Christian environment and went to church since childhood but I still had fears and emptiness inside. One night, during a Christian camp, we listened to a talk on 'The Gospel'. Afterwards, my mind was full of thoughts, I couldn't sleep and felt a nudge to pray.

As I prayed the Holy Spirit helped me and my heart was opened. I was reminded of the importance of having a relationship with Jesus. Knowing him from a distance is not enough, I need to follow him. My attitudes changed slowly, and I started to live not only for myself but to be a blessing for others. Since then my heart has been growing with passion to share about Jesus. The Holy Spirit guides me and helps me live life God's way.

Words from the Bible

> 'But when he, the Spirit of truth, comes, he will guide you into all the truth.'
>
> **John 16:13**

As well as the Bible, the Holy Spirit will lead us on our journey. We know we belong to God because of the Holy Spirit in us. He guides us about what is right and wrong. This often happens through a deep sense of conviction about what is wrong and, conversely, an incredible peace about what is right.

You will learn more about this the longer you are on the journey, so keep going.

Words to Pray

Thank you, God, for your Holy Spirit. Teach me to know when your Holy Spirit is leading me to what is right for me to do. May your Holy Spirit give me the strength I need to live my life for you. Help me to know and feel you are there. Amen.

30 The Journey

Your Thoughts

Scan on your smartphone or tablet to help you discover more.

DAY 7

Telling other people

32 The Journey

It's good to tell other people that you have become a Christian. This is called 'witnessing' or 'being a witness'. A witness tells of their personal experience. That's all you have to do. Talk about your good news of becoming a Christian.

Tell your Christian friends or someone at the church you are attending first – they can give you a few tips. This will give you confidence to tell your family and friends who don't know Jesus.

Phil's Journey

As a new Christian, my biggest challenge was telling the players at Nottingham Forest I had signed for Jesus. I thought the lads wouldn't understand.

Stuart Pearce found out and asked me in front of all the players, 'What's this about you becoming all religious?' I took a deep breath and told them all about it. It was such a relief. I had got myself worked up over nothing.

My confidence grew and now it's an integral part of my faith. I now know the importance of sharing my faith to try and help people understand the reality of Jesus.

Words from the Bible

> 'But you will receive power when the Holy Spirit comes on you; and you will be my witnesses in Jerusalem, and in all Judea and Samaria, and to the ends of the earth.'
>
> Acts 1:8

Telling people about God encourages you in your journey and helps others on their journey too. I feel closest to God when I am sharing my faith – it just does something for me as I speak about God.

You will learn more about this the longer you are on the journey, so keep going.

Words to Pray

Thank you, God, for what you have done for me. Help me to know what to say to people about you, and give me the boldness and confidence I need to say it. Amen.

Your Thoughts

Scan on your smartphone or tablet to help you discover more.

DAY 8

Keep on, keeping on

Being a Christian isn't always going to be easy. There may be times when you want to give it all up. You are not on your own, we all feel like that from time to time. Even if you weren't a Christian, life wouldn't always be easy; but as a Christian, God is always with you.

Tell God and your Christian friends when you are finding it tough. There will likely be someone in your church community who has experienced what you are going through. Let them support you and share with you.

Nitasha's Journey

Before I became a Christian, everything seemed like non-stop drama. I was spiralling out of control! I cared for nothing bar survival and success. So many mistakes. All the heartache and turmoil became too heavy to do life within my own strength. Accepting Christ into my heart was the very beginning of a relationship that led to healing, peace, a purpose revealed, releasing, discovery, and a deeper understanding of so much more. Choosing to continue this journey with him, allows for me to grow under his protection and guidance. How much more does he have in store for you?

Words from the Bible

> 'God has said, "Never will I leave you; never will I forsake you."'
>
> Hebrews 13:5

God does what he promises. There will be times on your journey when you feel distant, but one thing is definite: God promises to stay with us and that's what he will do. You may not be able to see it at the time and you may question whether he is really there, but he is and you will be able to look back and see that he was.

You will learn more about this the longer you are on the journey, so keep going.

Words to Pray

Thank you, God, that you have promised to be with me always. Help me to believe it even when I go through tough times. I also ask that you would help me to never leave you. Amen.

38 The Journey

Your Thoughts

Scan on your smartphone or tablet to help you discover more.

Final words

Joy in the journey

I hope that you have found this book helpful in the very early stages of your new-found faith. You will have learned throughout it that being a Christian is all about **belonging, believing and behaving.**

Belonging to God and his family, which is amazing. What an identity: you are one of God's children and you get to travel this world in that knowledge with a bunch of people who also know it.

Believing and trusting in God however you feel. Pray each day that God would strengthen your faith in him and your knowledge of him through prayer, reading the Bible and being part of a local church.

Behaving like someone who is a Christian. When you become a Christian, it changes the way you think and act. Some change is immediate; some takes longer. But as we choose to live life God's way and not ours it shows to others that God not only rescues us, he transforms lives.

Keep journeying, and help others on their journey. That's where the joy is.

Mark

Mark Greenwood

Also available

Big Yes, Little Yes, Healthy Maybe
ISBN 978-1-9997161-3-4

Big Yes, Little Yes, Healthy Maybe Study Guide
ISBN 978-1-910719-92-3

Now that is a good answer!
ISBN 978-1-904726-81-4

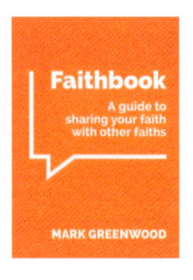

Faithbook
ISBN 978-1-914388-16-3

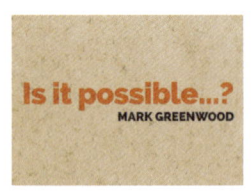

Is it possible...?
ISBN 978-1-914388-10-1

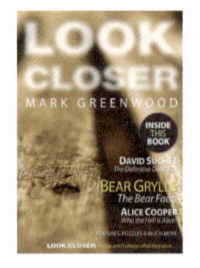

Look Closer
ISBN 978-1-914388-15-6

To buy these and other resources to help you along the journey visit **revmarkgreenwood.com**